T0040493

THE SHACK

THE SHACK

Irish Poets in the Foothills and Mountains of the Blue Ridge

WAKE FOREST UNIVERSITY PRESS

Wake Forest University Press
Post Office Box 7333
Winston-Salem, NC 27109
WFUPRESS.WFU.EDU

POEMS AND PROSE © Paul Muldoon, Eiléan Ní Chuilleanáin, David Wheatley,
John Montague & Elizabeth Wassell, Vona Groarke, Ciaran Carson,
Medbh McGuckian, Conor O'Callaghan, Michael Longley, and Derek Mahon

WATERCOLORS © Kenneth Frazelle

Salem from the Southwest (1824) and *Self-Portrait* by Christian Daniel Welfare
© the Museum of Early Southern Decorative Arts (MESDA) at Old Salem

Library of Congress Catalog Number 2014954158
ISBN 978-1-930630-71-0

Designed and set in Verdigris
by Nathan W. Moehlmann,
Goosepen Studio & Press

Printed on acid-free paper
in the United States of America

The editors are grateful to THE BOYLE FAMILY FUND
for its generous support in the publication of this book

for

DILLON & GUINN

Contents

Preface

THE BEGINNINGS OF Wake Forest University Press are both moving and curious, as Dillon Johnston, the founder — who remains an advising editor — describes them: "Our press began in 1974 when I met with Edwin Wilson, the provost of Wake Forest University, where I was teaching literature. Before approaching him, I had written an essay on Irish poetry for *Shenandoah* for which I had had great difficulty finding the poets' books (all three or four people I talked with at Oxford University Press in New York could not find Seamus Heaney on the Oxford list). Provost Wilson, remarkable for his balance of kindness and judgment, recognized the publishing need and agreed that universities should contribute to, as well as be repositories for, literature."[1]

Edwin Wilson also remembers the project: "It was obviously our chance to fill a gap.... I knew that Dillon had good judgment and was familiar with the tradition of Irish poetry, and I was impressed by his willingness to devote energy and time to the experiment. Besides, it seemed natural for us to develop this as a special project, since our library has been building a good collection of materials for Irish studies."[2]

Wilson's literary acumen and support has been vital to the Press for many years. Though he is now retired, he remains an indefatigable advocate. Johnston recognizes his help and insight from the early days: "[Wilson] helped me refine my proposal to create a press specializing in Irish poetry, and sent me to Ireland for five weeks. There, in the Trinity College and National libraries," writes Johnston, "I read all the back issues of *Poetry Ireland* and *The Honest Ulsterman*, and possibly all of the other literary journals published in Ireland at that time. In Dublin I met Liam Miller, the heroic founder of the Dolmen Press; Tom and Eleanor Kinsella; Peter Fallon, founder of The Gallery Press; and other poets and editors. In Belfast, I met Jim and Diane Gracey, the directors of Blackstaff Press; the poets Paul Muldoon, Frank Ormsby, and Michael Longley; and Michael's wife Edna, a literary and cultural critic. In Dublin, when evenings were devoid of hospitable poets, I would marinate my notes and ideas at my lodgings in Kelly's Hotel, in its final unregenerate year as after-hours drink-house for the police and other insomniacs. Before leaving Dublin, I wrote to Charles Monteith at Faber and Faber with the hope of meeting him on my return through London, but he told me, quite understandably, that he saw no basis for a meeting or for assuming I could get a press into efficient gear."

Johnston proceeds to lovingly describe the comical launch of the Press: "[Monteith] would not have been reassured by the Press's inauguration in March of 1976, which is suffused with sweet embarrassment in my memory. Eight cases of home-brewed stout, capped with extra sugar to raise the alcohol content, had detonated in my basement during a week-long cannonade, from which Bill Moss, Richard Murdoch, and I ('the Press') rescued five cases. This stout, along with Irish coffees spiked with Irish whiskey bootlegged from Washington, D.C., converted the normally genteel late-afternoon audience at the Reynolda House museum into a good imitation of Kelly's after-hours clientele. After Kevin Sullivan and John Rees Moore delivered introductory comments, Liam Miller, whose indisputable genius for book design and innovative publishing did not extend to oratory, lulled the audience into a soft stupor. Having mollified his own stage-fright by visits to the kitchen — 'Another Irish coffee, but hold the coffee' — he took the audience's susurrus as sounds of approval and spoke for nearly an hour. Whispered reports that our university's president was safely asleep allowed me to catch my breath." Johnston quips how the press "began tiny and grew to be small." Yet because of its editorial prerogatives, it remains the major publisher of Irish poetry in North America.

From its foundation, the mission of Wake Forest University Press has been to introduce Irish poetry to an American audience. Johnston comments on the relationship of American readers to Irish poetry: "American readers seem attracted to poetry that is thoroughly grounded in a fully explored and therefore small space, such as Patrick Kavanagh's parish or even W. B. Yeats's 'little room.' This American audience comes from someplace, an urban enclave or a rural village, the boundaries of which get blurred by or absorbed into the continental media or the not-quite-imaginable concept of 'America.' In Ireland, the localities in which Irish poetry takes root were federalized and imprinted with their identity by the emergence of the Dolmen Press in the 1950s and The Gallery Press under Peter Fallon in the early 1970s. If the confidently localized poetry of Ireland appeals to

Americans, who are necessarily but to varying degrees displaced, then, conversely, we might wonder about the impact of this wider American audience on Irish poets and poetry."

Johnston remembers a specific illustration in 1980, when "Wake Forest had just published Paul Muldoon's *Why Brownlee Left* and anticipated the publication of Michael Longley's *Selected Poems 1963–1980*." In the spring of 1980, these two poets came from their Belfast homes to New York's Public Theater to launch Wake Forest's publication of these two books. Johnston, his wife and fellow publisher, Guinn Batten, and Muldoon and Longley slept on the floor of a friend's apartment on the edge of Harlem, and took a two-day trek around the city, from bookstores to the St. Thomas Choir School for a discussion of poetry, to the celebrated Public Theater for Muldoon's and Longley's first Manhattan reading. Johnston describes the night with his usual self-deprecating irony: "[The night] plays back in my memory as a poet's version of the Beatles' accelerated film *A Hard Day's Night* — without the soundtrack of screaming girls, of course. The reading itself was successful by any standard: the sale of many books, moving and effective readings, thunderous applause and warm laughter from the large audience. The oddity of the lighting, however, persists in my memory. Although the laser-like spotlighting must have left this audience with nearly photographic images of these two poets, the house itself was cast into such a Stygian darkness that, with no reception or book signing after the reading, this responsive audience remained absolutely faceless to these poets."

"In a more general sense," Johnston continues, "this scenario might characterize the relation of Irish poets to North American audiences in 1980. Whereas the poetry had begun to win a readership through course adoptions, annual or biennial reading tours by most of the poets, and some direct responses to brochures, other advertising, and reviews, the major Irish poets — excepting Thomas Kinsella and occasionally Richard Murphy — remained in Ireland and directed their poetry toward an Irish and, to a lesser extent, English audience." This was not to remain the case in the lives of subsequent generations, however. The influence of American poetry as well as its culture would permeate the literary scene in Ireland. For Seamus Heaney, Derek Mahon, and Paul Muldoon in particular, the relationship between the United States and Ireland would be an intimately lived if not an uncritical one. Heaney would teach at Berkeley temporarily, then later take on a full-time position at Harvard, and go on to win the Nobel Prize in Literature. Mahon taught at New York University and spent much of the 1990s in Greenwich Village, an experience recorded into his marvelous volume *The Hudson Letter* (1996). Paul Muldoon now teaches at Princeton.

For Muldoon and Mahon, Wake Forest provided one of the initial entries. Mahon's poem "The Globe in Carolina" (originally called "The Globe in North Carolina" and published by Wake Forest University Press in the 1982 volume *The Hunt By Night*) was written while Mahon was teaching a summer class at Wake Forest. Mahon was at Wake Forest because of his relationship with WFU Press, and his friendship with Dillon and Guinn. Beginning with the image of a globe spinning at the poet's touch, the poem is a contemplation of his life divided between Ireland and the United States, and a meditation on the relationship between earth and sky as well as that between the large open spaces and "substantial cities" of the U.S. It is a poem caught between the luxuriance of nature in America and the kitsch of its society, all the while repeatedly aware of the yearning of the spirit for a universal thread, for the "night-sky" that is above the two halves of the imagined globe and which links two lovers on either side of the Atlantic. In "The Globe in Carolina," the poet attends both the personal and the universal as he considers the paradox of the increasingly interconnected though isolating and "lonesome" world in which we live. The poem has been frequently anthologized, and remains — after more than forty years — a strikingly elegant depiction of place and displacement, nostalgia and escape, of loss and longing. It is a "theoptic" reflection on the sidereal realm that revolves above our spinning "great mother" earth.

The intricate and at times intimate relationship between Ireland and the United States culminates perhaps in the career of Muldoon, for not only would he take up residence here, he would become a citizen. As with Derek Mahon and later Conor O'Callaghan and Vona Groarke, Wake Forest University played a small but significant role. In the poem "Promises, Promises," Paul Muldoon is in the tobacco country of North Carolina. The poem begins in the foothills, the Piedmont of the Blue Ridge, where Wake Forest University is located, then moves east to the coastline where, in Muldoon's imagination, Sir Walter Raleigh, who never actually came to

North America though he commissioned the expeditions here, is described as landing with a band of eighty whom he then left behind when he sailed for England. This group became the famous "lost colony" at Roanoke.

The disappearance of this colony has always haunted the American imagination, and it becomes a large part of Muldoon's cosmology in his subsequent poetry. When Raleigh returns, the colony is gone, but he does see "one fair hair in her braid" and "blue in an Indian girl's dead eye."

The image of a mixed breed has been important to Muldoon for metaphysical as well as cultural reasons. The dream of racial mixing contains various hopes and parallels: a hope to transcend the conflicts that would engulf the Indians and whites as the United States formed, and a keenly felt parallel between the Irish and American Indian experience of colonization and dispossession. A balance between places is struck, but one wonders whether the promise, of love, of the new world, will be fulfilled.

The poems and reflections that come between these two poems by Muldoon and Mahon are a conversation in poetry and prose across a wide array of circumstances and decades, which was generated by Dillon Johnston's bold venture in launching an Irish poetry press at Wake Forest University in Winston-Salem, North Carolina. Many of the poets have provided a commentary on their work that uncovers the genesis of the poem and/or describes the background. Eiléan Ní Chuilleanáin begins her poem, "The Copious Dark," with a long-remembered image from her first trip to Winston-Salem many years ago. David Wheatley, who has visited and read at Wake Forest more than once, writes of his discovery of North American "avian forms." John Montague, whose volume *A Slow Dance* was WFU Press's first book in 1975, and his wife, Elizabeth Wassell, charmingly look back at their visit with Johnston and Batten in the Virginia mountains, calling Johnston "a scholar and a gentleman." Their remembrance is followed by Vona Groarke, who co-held the poet-in-residence position at Wake Forest in the mid–2000s and who poetically depicts the pleasures and pitfalls of adapting to life in America. Ciaran Carson has been with WFU Press since 1976 and has been deeply connected to both the Press and Johnston's tenure as director. He is not only a poet but also a renowned traditional musician and music historian who fondly and humorously recalls listening to mountain music with Johnston and Batten. Another long-time Wake Forest poet who also has visited here often, Medbh McGuckian recollects touring Old Salem, the restored Moravian village, with Candide Jones, who was the assistant director of the Press for many years. Conor O'Callaghan, one of the last poets Johnston signed to the WFU Press roster before his retirement, remembers his first meeting with Johnston and his several years teaching at Wake Forest. And in this volume's title poem, "The Shack," Michael Longley reminisces on his experience with Johnston and Batten in their mountain-top cabin.

The complex relationship between the Appalachians and Ireland has long been noted, but seldom so personally and artistically as in this book. Beginning with a reverie in the foothills, moving through meditations on nature and culture and on the old world meeting the new, and ending with a hand spinning a globe in Carolina, these poems and reflections bring with them a transatlantic consciousness that has increasingly come to define our lives. Not only did Wake Forest University Press bring the globe to Carolina, but also, in its way, introduced Wake Forest University to the world.

1. Johnston, Dillon, "Wake Forest University Press: Some Reflections," *Princeton University Library Chronicle* LIX (1997–1998): 581–594. All subsequent quotations from Johnston are from this publication.

2. McIntyre, Deni, "The Wake Forest University Press: Irish books in American covers — nine volumes and going strong," *Wake Forest Magazine* (Spring 1980): 29–30.

THE SHACK

Watercolor by Kenneth Frazelle

Promises, Promises

I am stretched out under the lean-to
Of an old tobacco-shed
On a farm in North Carolina.
A cardinal sings from the dogwood
For the love of marijuana.
His song goes over my head.
There is such splendour in the grass
I might be the picture of happiness.
Yet I am utterly bereft
Of the low hills, the open-ended sky,
The wave upon wave of pasture
Rolling in, and just as surely
Falling short of my bare feet.
Whatever is passing is passing me by.

I am with Raleigh, near the Atlantic,
Where we have built a stockade
Around our little colony.
Give him his scallop-shell of quiet,
His staff of faith to walk upon,
His scrip of joy, immortal diet —
We are some eighty souls
On whom Raleigh will hoist his sails.
He will return, years afterwards,
To wonder where and why
We might have altogether disappeared,
Only to glimpse us here and there
As one fair strand in her braid,
The blue in an Indian girl's dead eye.

I am stretched out under the lean-to
Of an old tobacco-shed
On a farm in North Carolina,
When someone or other, warm, naked,
Stirs within my own skeleton
And stands on tip-toe to look out
Over the horizon,
Through the zones, across the ocean.
The cardinal sings from a redbud
For the love of one slender and shy,
The flight after flight of stairs
To her room in Bayswater,
The damson freckle on her throat
That I kissed when we kissed Goodbye.

~ EILÉAN NÍ CHUILLEANÁIN ~

The Copious Dark

She used to love the darkness, how it brought
Closer the presence of flesh, the white arms and breast
Of a stranger in a railway carriage a dim glow —
Or the time when the bus drew up at a woodland corner
And a young black man jumped off, and a shade
Moved among shades to embrace him under the leaves —

Every frame of a lit window, the secrets bared —
Books packed warm on a wall — each blank shining blind,
Each folded hush of shutters without a glimmer,
Even the sucked-sweet tones of neon reflected in rain
In insomniac towns, boulevards where the odd light step
Was a man walking alone: they would all be kept,

Those promises, for people not yet in sight:
Wellsprings she still kept searching for after the night
When every wall turned yellow. Questing she roamed
After the windows she loved, and again they showed
The back rooms of bakeries, the clean engine-rooms and all
The floodlit open yards where a van idled by a wall,

A wall as long as life, as long as work.
                              The blighted
Shuttered doors in the wall are too many to scan —
As many as the horses in the royal stable, as the lighted
Candles in the grand procession? Who can explain
Why the wasps are asleep in the dark in their numbered holes
And the lights shine all night in the hospital corridors?

THIS POEM WAS A LONG TIME in gestation. It started from a journey I took on a Greyhound bus. It was 1977, my first time touching the edges of the Western hemisphere. I had had serious doubts about the existence of land across the Atlantic and they had not really been allayed by the plane's long slow descent over, it seemed *into*, the sea, that ended by skimming the tops of waves and then pretending to land on solid ground. I took a train to Baltimore and was somewhat reassured, though bothered by the amount of wilderness on show, and how it alternated with the human settlement: forest, then suburb and then forest and then industry.

Next day, I got on a series of buses, and when the first one headed out into Maryland and afterwards down the Shenandoah valley, I saw fields with cows and horses, houses in the countryside with long verandas on which ancient men cuddled their shotguns, towns with the names of battles where people sat in the sun on the steps of the county jail. This was undoubtedly a real place. Even if some of my memories are skewed I am quite sure of the sensation of saying to myself, 'This place exists after all, other people have seen it before me, they live here and it is strange'. I sat up at the front of the bus and let the colours of field and barn crowd into my head. Then there was a wait in a bus station where people were poor, and smoked.

In the second bus the driver talked to an old woman who was going all the way to Alabama. They told each other some of the most wonderful stories I've ever heard, and I have never been able to write about them, but perhaps some day I will. In the third bus it was evening, and we were crossing into North Carolina. I wasn't noticing the other travellers, and the landscape was darkening. Somebody was talking about how wonderful the foliage had been last week. Then the bus drew up at a crossroads corner just as it got really dark, and the fact that we were very near some tall trees made it seem even darker. A young, very graceful black man jumped from the bus with a small bundle on his shoulder, and a girl who had been waiting, invisible in the darkness of the trees, moved into the half-light to embrace him. I saw Orpheus and Eurydice meeting in the underworld.

At once I knew that this was the high point of my journey, which had been exciting enough up to that moment. The stories, the landscape, were complete and real, but I was a casual visitor not connected in any way. In the evening bus I was so close to that meeting, nobody else could see it from my angle — or indeed perhaps from any angle. I felt my solitude and their coupleness. I felt then, all in a bundle, many ideas about how darkness and light interlock, all the gradations of light from the calm of an evening almost becoming night to the harsh glare of the operating theatre, how they show us each other, how we shrink from being shown, how they tell us about isolation and closeness, about interiors and desolate outsides.

Years later I wanted to write a poem that started from seeing a group, five or six migrant labourers, waiting near dawn beside an enormous motorway bridge in Sicily for a van to pick them up and take them to some exploitative toil. I imagined factories and warehouses I had seen, their outsides, long and windowless. As I moved memories about in my head, that moment on the bus came again, and I saw that what I had been struck by then was so complex because there hovered in the background the dreadful side of work, how work tears people away from their affections so that they become spies on the imagined happiness of others, the ones who sit in sunlight on the steps of the jail. That is one side of the poem, the unfairness between men and women, the awful appetites of the work machine, the way it devours our time and sends us to places that are filled with uneasy switchings between light and dark. The bundle of emotions finally began to unravel and I picked up the trailing ends and matched them as best I could. That evening in 1977, I was far from home, and lonely, reliving my student anguish in Oxford. But I was also full of energy, the energy of work and travel, and full of belief in the time of timetables, that I was really going to Winston-Salem and that Dillon Johnston would be meeting the bus.

— *Eiléan Ní Chuilleanáin*

A Shrike

Viscera of broken song
threading the knots in her butcher's call
to barbed wire, steel-strung
death's-head chorus giving tongue
to the music of each catch, each kill.

ROYGBIV

Carolina sky a paintball canvas where I traced
each last stripe on each last painted bunting's rainbow breast.

IF SYNAESTHESIA ASSUMED AVIAN FORM, it would be a painted
bunting, most rainbow-like of birds. Alas, I have never seen a painted
bunting and probably never will. There is an Arthur Rainbow in
Nabokov's *Lolita*, whose approximation to the great French poet's name
has the advantage of an implied allusion to his synaesthesic sonnet *'Voyelles'*
(*'A noir, E blanc...'*). I have seen an Eastern bluebird in North Carolina, which
manages a few at least of those rainbow colours, and also a shrike, though
not that bird's celebrated skewering of its prey on branches and barbed wire.
For a poet of the natural world, geography is destiny. Viktor Shklovsky said
that even if Tolstoy had never been born, someone else would have written
War and Peace instead; but if Elizabeth Bishop had been born in the Isle of
Wight, would 'The Moose' have been about a weasel or a water vole run-
ning in front of a bus instead? Bishop's bus passengers are country folk who
must have eaten their share of moose burgers in their time, but faced with
this sudden visitation they react with something like reverence ('Curious
creatures', 'Look at that, would you'). A fake or willed poem — trading on
what Beckett would call the *facultatif* — bears the same relationship to the
real thing as seeing a captive animal or bird does to a sighting in the wild, as
eating a creature does to watching it vanish into the woods.

I have never seen a painted bunting, though I did once see a tree come
alive at dusk on the Pacific Australian coast with a host of rainbow-coloured
lorikeets. I think my single favourite line of poetry is from George Oppen's
'Psalm', where he says of a group of deer he is watching 'That they are there!'
They are 'there' and there is nothing more to say. Sylvia Plath, who wrote a
poem about the shrike, implicitly addresses that enthusiastic destroyer of
small furry and feathered animals, Ted Hughes, in 'Pheasant', with its glo-
riously pacific and Oppen-resembling last line: 'I trespass stupidly. Let be,
let be.' I would rather see a painted bunting than write about it, but will set-
tle if needs be for a 'sighting' of the bird's absence in the form of a poem. A
memory and a memory of a dream are the same thing, Yeats said, and per-
haps a painted bunting and a (verbally) painted bunting eventually blur into
the same thing, in the eye of the mind at least. 'Gaudy flasher; red, blue,

green; what a whisk!' says Edwin Morgan of the species in his poem 'A Trace of Wings'. Where such revelations are at stake, it is easier than usual not to see and still believe, on the understanding — here, there, somewhere, any-where — 'That they are there!'

— *David Wheatley*

A Stoots Remembrance

FOR WRITERS WHO ARE NOT from the American South, to go there is almost a pilgrimage. From Faulkner onwards, the oblique, lyrical, even mystical Southern voice has called to us, and so to visit the towns and landscapes which have fostered it is particularly moving.

And combining that pilgrimage with friendship is a special privilege, as embodied in Stoots Mountain. That house, a bohemian, scholarly and poetic refuge, shines in our memory. Uproarious meals, long chats, the smell of wood and earth and innumerable flowers, even the walk to the outside lavatory beneath cold hard stars....

Once we were lost on the way to a neighbour's house. The path seemed to curve endlessly, with slopes rising and falling on all sides. Vines looped, leaves rustled, birds flapped suddenly out of the undergrowth. It was a beautiful afternoon, but we were afraid of dogs, shotguns, men in trucks, the perilous-looking gorge with its rush of water. Anything might happen.

And then we turned a corner, and there they were, Dillon's neighbours, standing on a lawn, laughing, and drinking from tall glasses. And there was Dillon himself, on a swing beneath a venerable tree, flying back and forth, up and down, a scholar and a gentleman, but also like a child.

The Small Hours

A joyrider rips up Lockland.
It takes barely five minutes
for a Precinct helicopter
to dip and swivel over lawns
and two opposing lines of cars
parked innocently snug to the sidewalk.
They haven't found him yet.
Every couple of minutes or so
my blind soaks in outrageous light
and the helicopter hauls its drone
and feud all over my backyard.
There's a fan over my bed
that says similar things in summer:
adages, reproach and rhetoric.
I talk too much; give far too much away.
In mumbling my company I reckon on
a two-fold pay-off: some echo;
being found out, consequence.
I lie low. Minutes swell.
He must be out there somewhere,
lights switched off, crouched and bundled,
foot within an inch of the get-go.
I pull the comforter up over my ears,
count to forty-two, then start over.
I'm trying, hard and fast, to hold my breath.

Away

We have our own smallholding:
persimmon tree, crawl space, stoop,
red earth basement, ceiling fans, a job.

Hours I'm not sure where I am,
flitting through every amber
between Gales and Drumcliffe Road.

I paint woodwork the exact azure
of a wave's flipside
out the back of Spiddal pier

and any given morning pins
a swatch of sunlight
to my purple shamrock plant.

My faithless heart ratchets
in time to slower vowels,
higher daylight hours.

I grow quiet. Yesterday
I answered in a class of Irish
at the checkout of Walgreen's.

I walk through the day-to-day
as if ferrying a pint glass
filled to the brim with water

that spills into my own accent:
pewtered, dim, far-reaching,
lost for words.

Y OU WOULDN'T EXPECT TO FIND a Drumcliffe Road in Winston-Salem. But then again, Kerensky Street also comes as a bit of a surprise. Not that it's not cosmopolitan, of course; it's just that the connecting lines are not always obvious. I don't know if Drumcliffe Road has a Yeats connection, but if not, that's a lucky accident if you happen to be an Irish poet, coming to settle in the town. Being a poet, you have to be alive to words, wherever they occur. Street signs, shop names, pizza sandwich boards worn by guys down on their luck on Silas Creek Parkway — all the words in all the places become a kind of background noise from which high notes emerge, like the hum of traffic on the Parkway or the clarion call of a train whistle in the dead of night.

We lived on Gales Ave: a little after we moved in, we began to hear the vowels in the place-name rearrange themselves as Gaels. I suppose it's the lot of the emigrant, really, to prospect the strange in a new home, hoping to find a nugget of the familiar, of the known. And Winston-Salem was certainly new to me. I'd lived in New York, Philadelphia, and San Francisco at various stages of my life, but Winston-Salem wasn't really like any of these, or at least, wasn't like them in any way I knew how to recognise. There weren't so many Irish people that my accent didn't get commented on, in a friendly way, in shops. Only there for two years, I never adopted a way of speaking that wouldn't mark me out as an immediate outsider, a 'blow-in': the alternative was to speak less, and more carefully, if I wanted to dodge the usual exchanges about wheretos and whytofores. I wanted to hold back the words for more particular enterprises: specifically, for poems.

About one third, the first third, of my collection *Spindrift* was written while I lived there. Of the two poems titled 'Away' in that book, the first comes closest to mining what it felt like to me to live there. The gorgeous exoticism of words I'd not rubbed up against before — persimmon, crawl space, stoop. My small attempts to insinuate my Irish home into this new place: paint colours and house plants; the street signs I would read into, and the shop names too (who'd have guessed why I always shopped in Walgreens instead of CVS?). I was lying low, holding my Irish breath, maybe not quite lost for words, but allowing them to surprise me, if and when they did. I like those poems and I'm glad I have them: they make those two years in

Winston-Salem available to me again. When so much of what happens becomes so much forgotten, it's a small, good thing to be able to call up that time and place, and to remember how useful it is for a poet sometimes to be just as far from one home as the other.

— *Vona Groarke*

Fiddlin' John's Big Gobstopper

IN THIS FILM ABOUT the people of the Appalachian Mountains there is a man who believes that only he, in the whole wide world, has found God. He sits on a swing seat on his porch, holding a hickory switch. God speaks through the antenna of the switch. The man holds it in his hands and asks it questions; it answers with a nod or quiver as it bends and listens to the source. It is his divining rod. He lives in a rusted corrugated-tin shack surrounded by a junk-strewn yard. He keeps the radio switched off except for the news, the happenings which give him intimations of Armageddon. For otherwise the radio brings music, the Devil's music, sin made audible.

Then there are the faith-healers, the speakers of tongues, the handlers of snakes, the drinkers of strychnine, who believe the Word has rendered them immune. Some of them allow music, but not the Devil's dance music, which overpowers you with jump and rhythm. The camera pans through a landscape of derelict farms and dirt roads and automobile graveyards and clapboard faith missions, till we at last get a glimpse of this Devil-music. The film crew has assembled a band on a mountain-side: an old fiddler in his seventies or eighties, and what look like various members of his extended family — a son, perhaps, playing a five-string banjo; maybe his cousin, playing an unorthodox style of bottle-neck guitar, left-handed, with the bottle-neck the 'wrong' way round; and two girls* in their thirties or forties, one playing a washboard, the other a broomstick one-string bass.

The fiddle-player holds the fiddle in the crook of his arm; his face is expressionless, deadpan. They are all expressionless, except for the disciplined energy of their hands. The energy comes from the line of the music, a force without crescendo or diminuendo; it follows its line until it finishes. If this is the Devil's music, then the Devil is a pragmatist: while the music exists, there is nothing better; it does not strive for a perfect state, nor intimate the sublime, but runs within an acceptance of the world as it is; it is true to what people are, and absolutely true to the musicians who are playing it. There is no deception, there are no histrionics, no acting-out of unfelt emotion. Because of these values, folk music is often perceived to be 'impersonal'; and the producers of the film seem to accord with this view, for the musicians, at the end of it all, are given no credit. They have become anonymous, or they are illustrations of a theme. The implication is that they are hillbillies, and one hillbilly is much the same as another.

So far as I know, these people do not call themselves 'hillbillies'; nor is their music so called, but is generally referred to as 'Old-time', or 'Old-timey'. I love Old-time music, but it is almost unperceived in Britain and Ireland, where it is thought to be 'Bluegrass'. Even in the USA its audience is limited: in a record store in Mount Airy, North Carolina — one of the centres of Old-time — I found some dozen tapes of this music among a hundred or so of Bluegrass. I bought the whole dozen, much to the bemusement of the owner. When he discovered I was Irish, he was even more perplexed.

Old-time has, it seems, redneck Dixie connotations which sit uncomfortably with the overriding commercialism of most American music. It is not music to be consumed, but to be played and danced to. Here, unlike Bluegrass, instrumental breaks are rare. The players start the tune together, and they stay together, and they all play the same tune a lot of times; yet each time round the tune is subtly different — not, perhaps, because the musicians make conscious variations, but because they play the tune that very way at that very time, and it is exactly true to life, which has no pre-determined score, but goes on from one split second to the next, driving through the now into the future. *Hillbilly?* Its sophistication is immense.

If Old-timey has frills, they are subliminal: little bowed grace notes, say, which lean into the rhythm; for the rhythm is the thing, which absolutely fulfils the music's purpose. Its purpose is to close the gap between the dancers and the dance; yet its wildness summons up the mountain-gaps and airy distances between the scattered settlements of Appalachia. It has a high lonesome note, a floating *cri de coeur* that longs to find a partner. It makes you want to dance.

I want to hear it so much that I rummage around and find one of the tapes I bought in Mount Airy. This is the Iron Mountain String Band:

Iron Mountain String Band
'Music From The Mountain'

The Iron Mountain String Band is a traditional, Old-time dance band. Their sound is powerful and driving, yet graceful and smooth. They are often seen at Southern music contests and at dances. The music on this tape is a good example of the pure Grayson County style which is still alive. We hope you will enjoy it.

NANCY BETHEL ~ BASS: Along with her husband, Nick, Nancy has played traditional music for years. The Bethels' outgoing hospitality is well known to those familiar with old time music competitions. Like the congeniality shown in the Bethel camp, Nancy's bass playing reflects the necessary give-and-take which makes up an Old-time band. Nancy is a resident of Selma, Virginia.

GENE HALL ~ GUITAR: Gene is the band's manager and co-ordinator. He gave the band its name because he lives near Iron Mountain and sees it every morning on his way to work. Gene's guitar playing reflects the image of the mountain — solid, strong and dependable. He lives with his wife, Anna Lee (a very fine spoon-player and flatfoot dancer), in the Elk Creek Community of Grayson County.

ENOCH RUTHERFORD ~ CLAWHAMMER BANJO: Enoch is well known for his pure, hard-driving, Grayson County banjo playing. His style clearly reflects his home community's name of Gold Hill in that, like gold, it is now very rare. Over the years Enoch has performed with the areas's best musicians. He has also been generous about passing along the tradition.

W. S. MAYO ~ FIDDLE: W. S. (Wiley) employs a unique underhanded Grayson County style of bowing which he learned from the late Albert Hash. He has always enjoyed playing Old-time dance tunes with other traditional musicians. Like the other band members, he is well known to be ready to play all day and all night. W. S. lives in Glade Spring, Virginia with his wife, Ray (who also plays clawhammer banjo).

DALE MORRIS ~ VOCALS: Dale is a well known and versatile local musician. Because of his natural feel and ear for traditional tunes, he is a great friend of Old-time musicians. He has graciously agreed to help the Iron Mountain String Band with the production and vocals of this tape. Dale lives in the Elk Creek Community with his family.

So I stick it into the sound system, and I'm writing this and tapping my feet to the great music when my four-year-old daughter, Mary, comes into the kitchen and starts to dance to it, for this is kitchen music, after all. I take her hands and dance with her and I forget the writing as we weave together in and out of time.

It brings to mind the time Dillon Johnston and Guinn Batten took me to a festival in West Virginia, where this brilliant Old-time band played on the back of a lorry, and old folk and young folk got up and danced as the fancy took them: this big farmer of an old guy partnering a little girl about my Mary's age, making delicate, floaty triplet steps with his yellow-laced big red boots in counterpoint to her petite feet. I can still hear the cluck and gurgle of the banjo, the lovely, scrapy rosiny push of the fiddle, nice little bass runs on the guitar picking out significant bits of rhythm … ridge after ridge, the mountains stretch away into the blue distance, and the memory of the Blue Ridge Mountains of Virginia blurs into the present as I listen to the Iron Mountain String Band for about the eighteenth time. It is the fifteenth of May, 1995, and the Band is playing some time in 1992, as recorded in a studio in Galax, Virginia, but I hear it different every time.

Compared to the baroque plethora of the Irish repertoire, American Old-time has relatively few tunes. Sets or medleys of tunes are rarely played, but the one tune is played many times. The playing is relatively unadorned: most of the work on the fiddle, for example, is done by the bow (though the left hand can be very subtle, making little off-beat finger-flicks against the bow, to give the note an edge). Yet, given these restrictions, the music is never boring, because it defeats time. The world beyond the tune moves to a different time. I've just counted how many times the Iron Mountain String Band play 'Sugar Hill' on a six-minute-long track, and it comes to fourteen, which is really twenty-eight, since the tune is doubled. This is a lot of times; but in real life, no one's counting — you lose track of numbers. You have to move to the music and be taken over by its mantra. In its circular reiteration and reprises, 'Old-time' is a paradox: it is not old, but of the here-and-now; its players constantly renew the breakdowns which have stood the clichéd test of time.

Old-time is not Bluegrass, and I am often bored by Bluegrass precisely because of its striving for newness and effect, its fussy, jazzy virtuosity. In Bluegrass, everyone must get a break, and because the breaks are predicated they tend to make the tunes they've taken in sound all the same, as the solo-ist goes through his formulae of variations. I generalise, of course, for Old-time and Bluegrass are not diametrically opposed, but are different shades of a spectrum that runs all the way to Country and back again.

Take the case of Fiddlin' John Carson, who is often represented as the man who started the Country music boom; equally, he can be credited as being the progenitor of Bluegrass. I first heard of Carson when I was in-troduced to the American musician Kenny Hall, some twenty years ago in Dublin. 'You're Carson?' he says. 'You must be something to Fiddlin' John.' It's possible. John Carson (and I used to have a mad Uncle John) was born on 23 March 1868 on a farm in Fannin County, Georgia. When he was ten years old, he inherited the fiddle his grandfather had brought over from Ireland. As a young man, he moved to the Atlanta area and worked as a race-horse jockey, among other things. Though not working regularly as a musi-cian at this time, he was already known as 'Fiddlin' John'. Here, as recorded in the *Radio Digest* of 7 November 1925, is how he got his name:

One of the most interesting memories in the vari-colored career of the Fannin County virtuoso is the fiddling contest at which the mountain boy outfiddled Governor Bob Taylor of Tennessee. This contest was the big event of the year. 'Fiddlin' Bob', as he was popularly known, was re-nowned for his skill on the fiddle, and few had ever been found who were near enough his level to make a competition interesting.

But on this momentous occasion, a new adversary was discovered. A hardy mountaineer was entered in the contest, who was the pride and hope of his friends who had come along with him to lend any moral support they could. The contest went on and it was a thrilling battle between the two fa-vourites — Governor Bob Taylor, and the unknown mountaineer. Then the finish and young Carson was declared winner and thereafter became known as Fiddlin' John, while Governor Taylor was so delighted with the young fellow's playing that right there on the spot, he bestowed his fiddle on the proud victor.

Carson soon became well known in the Atlanta area, playing as warm-up for travelling circuses and medicine shows; his ability to draw a crowd also led him into associations with some of Georgia's most distinguished politicians, who hired him to play and sing home-made campaign songs. However, his first record was not made until he was fifty-five, in June 1923; the industry was still in its infancy, and tended to be directed at a more affluent audience than those who would want to hear this style of music.

When the Okeh company issued 'The Little Old Log Cabin in the Lane/ The Old Hen Cackled and the Rooster's Going to Crow', it was an immediate hit, to the extent that Fiddlin' John declared he could nearly give up making moonshine. Others, equally successful, followed, and all in all he recorded some one hundred and fifty sides. What is interesting is the staggering diversity of the material. Fiddlin' John was promiscuous in his repertoire, which included old British ballads, blackface minstrel songs, Tin Pan Alley and Broadway hits, religious songs, blues ballads, Victorian parlour songs, songs written specially about topical events; he even recorded 'It's a Long Way to Tipperary'. And, of course, Old-time fiddle tunes, of which he was a master. What comes through in this *mélange* is Fiddlin' John's strength of personality and a directness and commitment of approach which could make any song his own.

In this, of course, he was not alone, for real folk singers never confined themselves to an academically-perceived 'folk' repertoire somehow fixed in amber, despite the depredations of the twentieth century: they sang what was in the air and adapted it to fit their own aesthetic. What unifies the material in Fiddlin' John's case is the impeccable phrasing, the underlying pulse in the grain of his voice going against the ostensible rhythm of the tune. At times he reminds me of the Northern Irish singer, the late Eddie Butcher; at others, the modern Country singer George Jones. I suspect Fiddlin' John could be all things to all men, and it is not surprising that he should be claimed by the followers of diverse genres. To me, he is old-time personified.

Fiddlin' John's first records were solo, with his own fiddle accompaniment; thereafter, he played with a band known as the Virginia Reelers, which included, among others, his daughter Rosa Lee, otherwise known as Moonshine Kate, and a fiddle-player called 'Bully' Brewer. The following exchange with 'Bully' takes place on 'OK 45448':

BULLY: I'm the best fiddler that ever wobbled a bow.

JOHN: I don't give a durn, I'm the best fiddler that ever jerked the hairs of a horse's tail across the belly of a cat.

BULLY: Well, I'll play 'Old Hen Cackle'.

JOHN: Turn your dog loose.

Bully plays

BULLY: Well, what're you going to play, John?

JOHN: I'm going to play the fiddle … that's a durn sight more than you've done.

Fiddlin' John Carson's success prompted other record companies to produce similar material, and it has been reckoned that some fifty thousand such records — 'Hillbilly', 'Country', 'Old-time', call it what you will — were issued, thus leaving an archive hardly matched by the efforts of serious field collectors. The companies, prompted by a purely commercial instinct, produced what local people wanted to hear, and rarely let their own preconceptions about music interfere: Fiddlin' John's producer, for example, thought his voice was 'pluperfect awful', but when he saw how the records sold, you may be sure he didn't arrange to have him take voice production lessons. In addition to the records, sheet music was produced to secure copyright and more dollars. Irene Spain, the stepdaughter of another OK artist, the Revd Andrew Jenkins, was hired to do the job on Fiddlin' John:

Fiddlin' John Carson's recording of 'You'll Never Miss Your Mother Until She's Gone' was the very first record I transcribed and 'I'm Glad My Wife's in Europe' was the second. Poor John couldn't make a record unless he was a little more than half drunk and he always had to have a 'jaw-breaker' — a candy ball about half as big as a golf ball — in his mouth and he would roll that around while singing. His words were so muddled up at times that we had to almost guess at what he was saying to get them on paper. Daddy (Jenkins) and my husband were both ministers and we were quite ashamed to be playing such records in our house for some of them were truly vulgar. But we would close the windows and doors and sit by the hours and sweat them out until we got them. Daddy, being blind, had a more sensitive ear than I, and he could understand words that I could not. So we worked together.

Such were the early days of the Country music business. When the Depression came, Fiddlin' John's music dropped out of favour and he hit hard times. However, when Eugene Talmadge, who knew Carson well, was elected Governor of Georgia, Fiddlin' John squatted in an elevator in the State Capitol and refused to budge until he got the job of running it. It reminds me of how the great *sean-nós* singer Joe Heaney worked as an epauletted doorman for a hotel just opposite the Dakota, where John Lennon was shot. The Governor saw to it that Fiddlin' John did get the job, and he worked there until a few weeks before his death on 11 December 1949. He was aged eighty-one. I was aged fourteen months. We live in each other's long shadows.

---

* *'Girl', latterly, has become the subject of a politically correct debate. In Ireland, the word is often used by women in referring to themselves, not disparagingly but to imply strength and individuality of character. I had the good fortune to be present when the great Tyrone singer Sarah Ann O'Neill first met the great Louth singer Mary Ann Carolan. She recognised her as a kindred spirit, for after Mrs Carolan had sung, Sarah Ann stood up and said, 'That girl there that just sung, would she sing another?' Mrs Carolan was in her seventies.*

Cape Fear Bank

   for Candide

Old world upland garden
in the new world. A snake-rail fence
and a live hedge of blood-twig
planted by Brother Christ, Brother Lung
and Brother August. Painted (in 1824)
by Christian Daniel Welfare.

In the medical, or hops garden,
last year's parsley, opium poppies
that wandered, true citron,
scurvy grass, hyssop,
blessed thistle (or St Mary's thistle),
muskmelons, lungwort,
wormseed or old woman,
the cockscomb and the apothecary rose.

Rose campion, the Cherokee rose,
spider flowers and four o'clocks,
Angel's trumpet, Joseph's Coat,
Joe Pye weed and johnny jump-ups,
Lamb's Ear along with Bachelor
Button. Late peaches with Bishop's
early peas. Oxheart carrots,
wren's egg and Rob Roy beans.

Tennisball and lazy lettuces,
vegetable oysters and tree peonies.
Globe amaranth and tassel hyacinth.
The blackhaw, bitternut and sourwood.
The mockernut, the Carolina allspice
(having the fragrance of strawberries),
the serviceberry, the Carolina silverbell.

The river birch and river plum,
box elder and shortleaf pine,
the honey locust and the black
locust tree, winged elm,
fringetree, all the oaks,
swamp, scarlet, pin and post.
Lantana and bottle gourd
vining the lower pleasure grounds
where one of my bee stands
began to swarm ...

According to the compass rose,
the furrow of the graveyard
uniquely is in blue,
and in Bethabara, house of passage,
an arbour of live cedars
had their tops chained together
into a green dome, had doors cut
through their branches
to grainfields of ancient spelt.

I AM REMEMBERING NOW the early love songs. Carolina moon keep shining, shining on the one I love. Sweet Caroline. In my mind I'm going to Carolina. This is reinforced by having just met Paul Simon at a gig in Dublin for Seamus Heaney!

Candide [Jones, Assistant Director of WFU Press] had brought me so kindly to visit an old Quaker style [Moravian] village where she also bought me a gift of a beautifully illustrated catalogue of the local herbs and therapeutic plants raised there. These names were themselves poetry, there was nothing to do but link them in an endless abundant list. Candide's adorable son's name [Daniel] is referred to. There is a delightful mix of sacred and profane love.

I was not yet to know that the voice of the monk-gardener here would so naturally conflate with the film-voice of Gregory Peck in the *Cape Fear* horror movie I watched long after. For there is no possible threat of violence to this peaceful Eden and although Greg and Veronique, who have both since sadly passed through the living house of passage, the poem that follows this in *The Book of the Angel* is about their Spanish/classical grounds in Beverley Hills with its swimming pools and tennis courts.

In both poems there is a desire to somehow symbolize the spirit paradise through examination of earthly heavens, of which Candide's house of hospitality and welcoming sunny lawns in Winston-Salem were and still are another pre-figuration.

— *Medbh McGuckian*

Salem from the Southwest *(1824) by Christian Daniel Welfare*

This

began with an Oriole pencil I stumbled on among the stalls
of Santa Monica and lost by lunch. It ends thus, and now.
For months there was a play on 'pastures new'
that became a blue sea that changed to something else.

There was something as well about the four walls
of a fortnight or three on the wagon. I'd forgotten also
an image of my gran in her kitchen up until a week ago,
the meadow of butterfly buns, her breathless 'It's very close'.

Then the night before last, after a few maudlin drinks,
I gave myself a table of pals dishing out seconds and thirds
and tippling till the cows come home and leaving the dinner things

for armchairs on the porch and a silence without words
that was nothing of the sort, thanks to this and thanks
to the darkness I threw in, littered with mockingbirds.

The Sun King

I wanted his sky-blue Ford, its sheetrock, its transmission issues.
I listened to his low-down yodelling skimming sunk studs
and snake rattles like wind chimes round his mantle in the hills
and parables waiting for windows to arrive where some lunchbox
was always asked what sort of lunchbox he took Roy for.
Le roi soleil.

       It stuck, from first coming with a bucket of mud
to the day of reckoning his lady friend brought marble cake
and Roy joined hands in a ring that all lost rooms be filled
by a sun to which even the godless among us could say Amen.

Then one afternoon *Leaves of Grass* fell onto the laminate.
The station wagon wasn't in the drive. The sprinklers,
for all the gilt and shadow in the street, had run dry.
My boy and girl were grown elsewhere. And somehow I,
five years east, woke in mind of an odd-job deity no heathen
need ever wake in mind of. King of sun, pray for me again.

Swell

Mid-March, on the daily a.m. drop-off
through a bunch of affluent side streets
between school and here

a refrigerated dairy produce truck
keeps catching almond and dogwood branches,
so much that blossoms blizzard

the windscreen and moonroof
and I have to switch the wipers
to intermittent in its slipstream.

All I mean to say is that it was lovely,
that not every given is bleak or wrong
and some even are as gorgeous as they are elementary.

The kids come home on different buses
the same shade of egg yolk.
We call my mother from the shore for Easter.

That truck and blossoms story gets longer,
hokier, with each retelling. I'm not bothered.
April's bright stretches, the mailman says, are swell.

Our local 'Y' widens its opening hours a smidgen.
The clay courts opposite pock and shuffle.
I learn to swim.

Woodsmoke

      I buy this woodstove
('Big Boy', Birmingham, AL)
      in a clearance sale
for the hut we're fixing up
at the top of the garden.

      For weeks all three-legs,
twenty-rusting-bucks of it
      hogs the patio.
It looks like some wild creature
in from the sticks to hunt scraps.

      Stock reports double
as tinder, TV listings,
      twigs the ice storm left
in its wake, war coverage
and a struck match. Flames bob up

      the split hotplate's cleft
like starlings newly hatched.
      I feed logs enough
to burn longer than I'll stand
and dawn blanches the embers.

      A month of woodsmoke.
The wardrobe reeks charred resin.
      The kids think I'm nuts:
their own hobo — duffel coat,
travel mug — states out the line.

Times I'll hum to it,
tell it stuff. It changes me,
        much as it changes
maple and newsprint to dust
gauzing porches, drifting blocks

        toward the highway,
the mall's afterglow, the sky.
        It halves the fallow
stretch from Xmas to Spring's boom.
Then the fire marshal stops by.

        It doesn't matter.
Since Daylight Savings happened
        the neighbours can rest.
Becoming is what matters,
the passage, the whetted axe.

        I get an odd peace
imagining these clear nights
        how bits of spare cash,
Alabama, this garden,
my son's and daughter's faces

        at the sliding door,
the market's ebbs, the stacked dead,
        a hut placed on pause,
its stove's words, my writing them,
the page's threshold even,

        this book in your hand,
the bookstore open Sunday
        in which you're reading,
are all bound to get threaded
through some flame's liminal eye.

I MET DILLON AT THE LAUNCH of Vona's first book, *Shale*. 1994, upstairs in Waterstones on Dawson Street in Dublin. I was hovering at the back after the readings when this guy approached and introduced himself: wiry, spectacled, soft-voiced, as hesitant as he was funny and he was plenty funny.

We didn't meet again until the end of that decade. 1999. After a different reading in the same venue, Peter Fallon [of The Gallery Press] said it looked likely Wake Forest would be doing a U.S. edition of my second book. Dillon called to our house in Dundalk later that year. We drank pints in The Spirit Store on the quays and put him on the express bus to Dublin. Back then, the Dublin express took two hours, stopping in every ditch along the old road. I remember Dillon pausing on the step onto the bus, turning to us and, with fear etched all over his features, asking: 'Does this bus have a john?' It did not. Dillon would later describe the journey, his bladder swelling with Guinness and the vehicle bumping off every pothole, as 'character-forming'.

Seatown and Earlier Poems (the title still makes me blush a bit) was launched at the first [Wake Forest] Irish Festival in March 2000. Dublin-LAX-Charlotte-Greensboro International. Dillon met me at the arrivals gate shortly before midnight. His place was a rickety thing with a porch on the aptly-named Shady Boulevard. Junkies, he assured me, regularly passed through his yard. Over a couple of pale ales, Dillon said I had a TV interview at 6 AM. Candide fetched me at 5.30 AM (the times are correct) and whisked me off to a balcony out the back of Graylyn House, where an African-American reporter thrust a mic in front of my trembling mouth and asked how super psyched I was to be an Irish poet, while a line of ceilidh dancers bopped around in the background. We did a reading that night, in the conservatory of Reynolda House. I remember leaning on the grand piano, knees knocking with nerves, while Dillon introduced me in terms so flattering as to render me unrecognisable to myself.

America can turn an Irish poet's head, if you're not careful. There is a great vignette in Foster's life of Yeats, where somebody recalls seeing Willie speak publicly shortly after returning from his first U.S. tour: Yeats had acquired, in the interim, a floor-length coat of emerald velvet and a mystical twinkle in his eye. He had, as we say, lost the run of himself.

At some point during that trip, Dillon mentioned an anthology of poems by Irish poets about North Carolina. He even told me one story, where he had mentioned the same possibility to another Irish who had been staying. The following morning, said poet was at Dillon's kitchen table in Shady Boulevard with a North Carolina poem he had written during the night. As you do. It was clear that the poem was a recycle, with local reference inserted at the top to justify inclusion in any such possible anthology. It started something like:

> As I sit at the breakfast table in North Carolina,
> I think of my dear old mum back in Cork …

In time, we would move there and I would write my own North Carolina poems, for their own sake, since the anthology seemed to have gone the way of most poetry ideas.

'This' was the earliest, and written long before we moved there. The sestet was composed quickly, shortly after returning from Winston in 2000. In my head was nothing more than the memory of laughing on Dillon's porch, with the lights of the downtown visible through trees in the background. The rest came piecemeal over the next year or so. 'The Sun King' happened long after we had left North Carolina. We had got an annex to our house on Gales converted into a sunroom. One of the workmen was called Roy and kept using the word 'lunchbox' as a synonym for 'dope'. He made me laugh. When they were done, he insisted we hold hands and thank Jesus. It was far more moving than I would have ever expected. The stove in 'Woodsmoke' was bought in an antiques store on West End Boulevard that was closing down. I got in touch with Wake's campus arborist, who gave me first dibs on all trees being felled. He would leave voice messages telling me the location of my latest pile of logs. I still have it: it got shipped over in 2008 and, as I type, is somewhere in my younger brother's stable in Ireland.

'Swell' was another of many American words that I loved. If I am completely honest, the word stuck in my head thanks to Jim Hans. I can still hear it in his Chicago accent. When I first interviewed at Wake, Jim had seemed a mean son of a bitch. But he turned out to be nothing of the sort.

Jim was the kindest, most supportive, and funniest colleague there. That needs saying, if just this once, and I dedicate this appearance of the poem to Jim by way of thanks. The blossoms belong to the Buena Vista neighbourhood, en route to Whitaker Elementary. The shore trip was thanks to Guinn and her family in Emerald Isle. The courts are those opposite the West End YMCA, where I did indeed take swimming lessons. I loved the noise of the 'burbs on early summer evenings. I wanted nothing more than to write something of that and of the hope implicit in that noise.

When did I last see Dillon? An MLA in Philly, over dinner in a restaurant named after Madame Blavatsky's white dog? Or during his sojourn in rural Missouri, when I became convinced that Dillon and Tony La Russa were twins separated at birth? Or a lugubrious lunch in Dublin, in that not remotely Yeatsian café The Winding Stair? I can hardly remember. Too long ago, anyway. Now and then I can hear him reading to me, shyly it seemed, a poem of his own in response to Muldoon's 'Quoof'. I still even chuckle at the thought of him shuffling to the gate of 'the shack', hands in pockets and eyes shark-dead, to ask: 'You boys lookin' for trouble?' I hope he is well wherever he is, still himself, and that our paths cross once more.

— *Conor O'Callaghan*

~ Michael Longley ~

The Shack

for Dillon & Guinn

I lie awake between the two sleeping couples.
Their careful breathing in the Blue Ridge Mountains
Disturbs me more than the engine ticking over
At the end of the lane, the repetitive whippoorwill,
The downpour's crescendo on corrugated iron.
Though there are no doors between them and me, perhaps
They will risk making love like embarrassed parents
While I remain motionless on my creaking divan.
They have shown me a copperhead, indian fire pinks
And buzzards like mobiles where the storm clouds hang.
I might as well be outside in the steamy field
Interrupting again the opossums' courtship,
Paralysing with torchlight pink noses, naked tails
Just beyond the shithouse where, like a fall of snow,
The equalising lime has covered our excrement.
Tomorrow when we pass the Pentecostal church
The wayside pulpit will read 'Thanks, Lord, for the rain.'

SOME OF THE HAPPIEST times of my life have been spent in the company of Dillon and Guinn, she effortlessly elegant, he charmingly ramshackle. I felt close to the soul of America when I stayed with them in their shack in the Blue Ridge Mountains among plants and animals new to me. In a spirit of loving reciprocity I rejoiced to introduce them to my own soul-landscape in County Mayo, the townland of Carrigskeewaun with its hares and stoats and otters. Edna, Guinn, Dillon, and I squelched across the salt marsh to the waterlily lake where rare orchids grow. I would share this place with hardly anyone else. Leaving Carrigskeewaun involves walking down a rocky path and wading through a tidal channel. In the darkness a wine-fuelled Dillon showed off. First, he vaulted a high galvanised gate, coming to a juddering halt. His judders went on for ages. Then he tried to perform his walking-on-water trick. He fell flat on his back in the channel's shallows and immediately began creating with his arms and legs what can only be called water-angels. Just in time we rescued his spectacles, a faint glimmer in the swirling sand. Wherever we are — in North Carolina or Missouri, in Belfast or County Mayo — we talk about the inner adventure of poetry. Dillon's shack reminds me of Ciaran Carson's belief that civilisation depends on what a few enthusiasts generate in small back rooms. To quote Derek Mahon, the shack was a place 'where a thought might grow'. Who is more thoughtful than Dillon? He is a visionary. Many Irish poets give thanks that he has so resolutely kept his head in the clouds.

— *Michael Longley*

52

~ DEREK MAHON ~

The Globe in Carolina

The earth spins to my fingertips and
Pauses beneath my outstretched hand;
White water seethes against the green
Capes where the continents begin.
Warm breezes move the pines and stir
The hot dust of the piedmont where
Night glides inland from town to town.
I love to see that sun go down.

It sets in a coniferous haze
Beyond Georgia while the anglepoise
Rears like a moon to shed its savage
Radiance on the desolate page,
On Dvořák sleeves and Audubon
Bird-prints; an electronic brain
Records the concrete music of
Our hardware in the heavens above.

From Hatteras to the Blue Ridge
Night spreads like ink on the unhedged
Tobacco fields and clucking lakes,
Bringing the lights on in the rocks
And swamps, the farms and motor courts,
Substantial cities, kitsch resorts —
Until, to the mild theoptic eye,
America is its own night-sky.

Out in the void and staring hard
At the dim stone where we were reared,
Great mother, now the gods have gone

We place our faith in you alone,
Inverting the procedures which
Knelt us to things beyond our reach.
Drop of the ocean, may your salt
Astringency redeem our fault.

Veined marble, if we only knew,
In practice as in theory, true
Redemption lies not in the thrust
Of action only, but the trust
We place in our peripheral
Night garden in the glory hole
Of space, a home from home, and what
Devotion we can bring to it.

You lie, an ocean to the east,
Your limbs composed, your mind at rest,
Asleep in a sunrise which will be
Your midday when it reaches me;
And what misgivings I might have
About the final value of
Our humanism pale before
The mere fact of your being there.

Five miles away a southbound freight
Sings its euphoria to the state
And passes on; unfinished work
Awaits me in the scented dark.
The halved globe, slowly turning, hugs
Its silence, while the lightning bugs
Are quiet beneath the open window,
Listening to that lonesome whistle blow.

Watercolor by Kenneth Frazelle

Contributors

KENNETH FRAZELLE was born in Jacksonville, North Carolina. He is a well-known composer whose work has included commissions from such renowned performers as Yo-Yo Ma, Dawn Upshaw, Paula Robison, tenor Anthony Dean Griffey, and the North Carolina Symphony. He was a student of Roger Sessions at the Juilliard School, and attended the North Carolina School of the Arts in Winston-Salem, where he now teaches. The Blue Ridge Mountains play an important part in many of his musical compositions and in his watercolors. He and his partner, Rick Mashburn, live in Winston-Salem and have a cabin on Stoots Mountain in Virginia.

CHRISTIAN DANIEL WELFARE (WOHLFAHRT) was a Moravian painter born in 1796 in Salem, North Carolina, where he received his education. In March 1824, Welfare went to Philadelphia and studied under the noted painter Thomas Sully. The subjects for his art were varied, and included reproductions of portraits of U.S. presidents and of famous religious canvases, portraits of Moravian worthies and their families, and watercolors of Salem streets and scenes. He died in Salem in 1840.

CIARAN CARSON was born and raised in Belfast, Northern Ireland. Educated at Queen's University Belfast, he was Chair of Poetry at its Seamus Heaney Centre for Poetry for ten years. He is a poet, a traditional musician, scholar of the Irish oral tradition, prose-writer, and translator. Wake Forest University Press has published fifteen of his volumes, beginning with *The New Estate* (1976), and including the groundbreaking *Belfast Confetti* (1989) and *First Language* (1994), which won the first ever T. S. Eliot Prize. Other titles include *Breaking News* (2003), which won the prestigious Forward Prize; *The Midnight Court* (2006), his rollicking translation of Brian Merriman's eighteenth-century Irish poem; *For All We Know* (2008); *Collected Poems* (2009); *In the Light Of* (2013), his renditions of Rimbaud's *Illuminations*; and *From Elsewhere* (2015), translations of and responses to the poetry of Jean Follain.

VONA GROARKE was born in Mostrim in the Irish Midlands and attended Trinity College Dublin and University College Cork. She co-held the Heimbold Chair in Irish Studies at Villanova University, and taught in the English Department at Wake Forest University for three years. Her poetry collections include *Shale* (1994), *Other People's Houses* (1999), and *Flight* (2002), shortlisted for the Forward Prize (UK) in 2002 and winner of the Michael Hartnett Award in 2003. Wake Forest University Press published *Flight and Earlier Poems* (2004), *Juniper Street* (2006), and *Spindrift* (2010). Her newest volume, *X*, was published in Ireland by The Gallery Press in 2014. She lives in Manchester, England, and teaches at the University of Manchester.

MICHAEL LONGLEY was born in Belfast and was educated at the Royal Belfast Academical Institution and Trinity College Dublin where he read Classics. He has published numerous collections of poetry including *Gorse Fires* (1991), which won the Whitbread Poetry Award, and *The Weather in Japan* (2000), which won the Hawthornden Prize, the T. S. Eliot Prize, and *The Irish Times* Poetry Prize. In 2001 he received the Queen's Gold Medal for Poetry, and in 2003 the Wilfred Owen Award. He was awarded a CBE (Order of the British Empire) in 2010 and was Ireland Professor of Poetry, a three-year appointment to be divided among Queen's University Belfast, Trinity College Dublin, and University College Dublin, 2007–2010. Wake Forest University Press has published ten of Longley's volumes, including his *Collected Poems* in 2007 and his most recent volume, *The Stairwell*, in 2014. He and his wife, the critic Edna Longley, live in Belfast.

DEREK MAHON was born in Belfast and was educated at Trinity College Dublin and at the Sorbonne in Paris. Wake Forest University Press published three of his volumes: *The Hunt by Night* (1982, redesigned in 1995), *The Hudson Letter* (1996), and *The Yellow Book* (1998), as well as his translation of Philippe Jaccottet's *Selected Poems* in 1988. He has written many volumes of poetry, translations and plays, and edited *The Penguin Book of Contemporary Irish Poetry* (1990) and *Modern Irish Poetry* (1972). His honors include the Irish American Foundation Award, a Lannan Foundation Award, a Guggenheim Fellowship, the American Ireland Fund Literary Award, the Arts Council Bursary, the Eric Gregory Award, and the David Cohen Prize for Literature.

MEDBH MCGUCKIAN was born in Belfast and is a graduate of Queen's University Belfast, with B.A. and M.A. degrees in English, and where she was the first woman to be named writer-in-residence. She now regularly teaches there. Volumes published by Wake Forest University Press include *On Ballycastle Beach* (1988), *Marconi's Cottage* (1992), *Captain Lavender* (1995), *Selected Poems* (1997), *Shelmalier* (1998), *The Soldiers of Year II* (2002), *The Book of the Angel* (2004), *The Currach Requires No Harbours* (2007), *My Love Has Fared Inland* (2010), and *The High Caul Cap* (2013). She lives in Belfast with her husband, John McGuckian.

JOHN MONTAGUE was born in Brooklyn, New York, and reared in County Tyrone, Northern Ireland. He was educated at University College Dublin, Yale University, and the University of Iowa. His first volume, *Forms of Exile*, appeared in 1959. Montague's *Collected Poems* was published in 1995, the same year he received the America Ireland Fund Literary Award. Wake Forest University Press has published his last ten volumes, including his most recent, *Speech Lessons*, in 2012. In 1998, he was named the first Ireland Professor of Poetry, a three-year appointment to be divided among Queen's University Belfast, Trinity College Dublin, and University College Dublin. His many awards include the Irish-American Cultural Institute's Award for Literature and a Guggenheim Fellowship. He divides his time between West Cork, Ireland, and France.

ELIZABETH WASSELL was born in New York, met John Montague in 1992 during a poetry reading, and they were married in 2005. She is the author of the novels *The Honey Plain* (1998), *Sleight of Hand* (1999), *The Thing He Loves* (2001), *Dangerous Pity* (2010), and *Sustenance* (2012). Her short stories have appeared in various publications, including the *Dublin Review* and *The Irish Times*.

PAUL MULDOON was born in County Armagh, Northern Ireland, was educated at Queen's University Belfast, and spent several years working for the BBC before moving to the United States. He now lives in New York City and holds the Howard G. B. Clark '21 Chair in the Humanities at Princeton University. He has been poetry editor of *The New Yorker* since 2007. Wake Forest University Press published four of his early volumes: *Mules* (1977), *Why Brownlee Left* (1980), *Quoof* (1983), and *Meeting The British* (1987). Other titles include *Madoc: A Mystery* (1992), *The Annals of Chile* (1994), *Hay* (1999), *Moy Sand and Gravel* (2004), *Horse Latitudes* (2006), *Maggot* (2010), and his most recent, *One Thousand Things Worth Knowing* (2015). He has received many awards and prizes, including an American Academy of Arts and Letters award in 1996 and the 2003 Pulitzer Prize.

Eiléan Ní Chuilleanáin was born in Cork, where she graduated
from University College Cork, with a B.A. in English and history, fol-
lowed by a M.A. in English. She later studied at Oxford. She was Associate
Professor of English, Dean of the Faculty of Arts (Letters), and a Fellow
of Trinity College Dublin until her retirement in 2011. She edits the lit-
erary journal *Cyphers* with two other poet-editors, including her husband
MacDara Woods. Wake Forest University Press has published eight of her
volumes, including *The Magdalene Sermon and Earlier Poems* (1991), *The Girl
Who Married the Reindeer* (2002), *Selected Poems* (2009), *The Sun-fish* (2010),
which was the winner of the International Griffin Poetry Prize, and *The
Legend of the Walled-Up Wife* (2012), translations from the Romanian poetry
of Ileana Mălăncioiu. Her most recent volume is *The Boys of Bluehill* (2015).

CONOR O'CALLAGHAN was born in Newry, Co. Down, Northern Ireland, and grew up in Dundalk, just south of the Irish border. He was educated at Trinity College Dublin and University College Cork. Wake Forest University Press published *Seatown and Earlier Poems* (2000), *Fiction* (2005), which was shortlisted for *The Irish Times* Poetry Now Prize, and most recently, *The Sun King* (2013), also shortlisted for the Poetry Now Prize. He is the editor of *The Wake Forest Series of Irish Poetry, Vol. III*. O'Callaghan has written widely on sport, especially soccer and cricket, and is the author of *Red Mist: Roy Keane and the Football Civil War* (2004). He co-held the Heimbold Chair in Irish Studies at Villanova University, taught in the English Department at Wake Forest University for three years, and currently teaches at Sheffield Hallam University in England.

DAVID WHEATLEY was born in Dublin and studied at Trinity College Dublin. He has published four collections with The Gallery Press in Ireland: *Thirst* (1997), which won the Rooney Prize for Irish Literature, *Misery Hill* (2000), *Mocker* (2006), and *A Nest on the Waves* (2010). With Justin Quinn he was a founder-editor of the poetry journal *Metre*. Wheatley was awarded the Vincent Buckley Prize in 2008, and his work has been featured in several anthologies, including *The Penguin Book of Irish Poetry*, *Identity Parade: New British & Irish Poets*, and *The Wake Forest Series of Irish Poetry, Vol. I* (2005). He is currently editing *The Wake Forest Series of Irish Poetry, Vol. IV*. He teaches at the University of Aberdeen in Scotland.

Notes & Acknowledgments

Notes on the watercolors:

My partner Rick Mashburn and I first drove up to Stoots Mountain with Guinn and Dillon on a late winter's day in 1984. We were all taken with its velvety tree-lined vistas and thrilling views. Being able to inhabit this place for decades has been rich and deeply affecting.

Hundreds of summer days have been filled with gardening, reading, calling the dogs, jotting down bird calls for music, and watercoloring the place's elusive light and weather. And those enchanting evenings with the four of us wrapped in conversation, wine, garlic, raspberries, and stars.

— *Ken Frazelle*

Acknowledgments:

"Promises, Promises" by Paul Muldoon was first published in *Why Brownlee Left* (1980, Wake Forest University Press) and is reprinted from *Poems 1968–1998* (2001, Farrar, Straus and Giroux) with the kind permission of the author and Farrar, Straus and Giroux.

"The Copious Dark" by Eiléan Ní Chuilleanáin from *The Sun-fish* is reproduced with the kind permission of the author and Wake Forest University Press.

"ROYGBIV" and "A Shrike" by David Wheatley are reprinted with the kind permission of the author.

"A Stoots Remembrance" by John Montague and Elizabeth Wassell appears with the kind permission of the authors.

"The Small Hours" and "Away" by Vona Groarke from *Spindrift* are reprinted with the kind permission of the author and The Gallery Press.

"Fiddlin' John's Big Gobstopper" by Ciaran Carson from *Last Night's Fun* is reproduced with the kind permission of the author and Macmillan.

"Cape Fear Bank" by Medbh McGuckian from *The Book of the Angel* is reproduced with the kind permission of the author and Wake Forest University Press.

"This" from *Fiction* and "The Sun King," "Swell," and "Woodsmoke" from *The Sun King* by Conor O'Callaghan are reproduced with the kind permission of the author and The Gallery Press.

"The Shack" by Michael Longley is reproduced from *Collected Poems* with the kind permission of the author, Jonathan Cape, and Wake Forest University Press.

"The Globe in Carolina" by Derek Mahon is reproduced from *New Collected Poems* with the kind permission of the author and The Gallery Press.

Watercolors by Kenneth Frazelle are reproduced with the kind permission of the artist (frazellewatercolors.blogspot.com).

Two paintings by Christian Daniel Welfare — *Salem from the Southwest* (1824), from the Museum of Early Southern Decorative Arts (MESDA) collection at Old Salem, and *Self-Portrait*, from the Wachovia Historical Society collection — are reproduced with the kind permission of MESDA.